MYSTERIES IN THE FOREST

STORIES OF THE STRANGE AND UNEXPLAINED

VOLUME 1

ERIK LAKE

FREE REIGN

ISBN 13: 979-8-89234-042-7

Free Reign Publishing, LLC
San Diego, CA

CONTENTS

1

BIGFOOT ENCOUNTER

Our story is one that intertwines love, nature, and an encounter so extraordinary, it seems lifted from the pages of folklore. My partner and I share a profound connection, not just with each other, but with the great outdoors. This connection was sparked under unusual circumstances in a remote forest, where fate brought us together as my car failed me in the middle of nowhere. Their timely arrival with friends on that day transformed a moment of distress into the beginning of a lifelong bond.

Over the years, our annual camping trips to that very spot became a sacred tradition, a cherished escape from our high-stress, fast-paced careers. Our approach to camping was intentionally simplistic; we sought the unadulterated embrace of nature, choosing the rugged confines of our SUV over the artificial shelter of tents. This nomadic style allowed us the freedom to traverse various trails, each day a new adventure, each night a different corner of the wilderness to call home. The stars and the moon were our constant companions, casting a serene glow over our nocturnal abode. And every trip culminated in spending a night at the very location where our paths first intersected, a spot that symbolized the serendipity of our union.

However, one particular trip veered into the realms of the unbelievable, altering our perception of the natural world forever. It was on the fifth night of this trip, a night that began like any other, under the tranquil canopy of the forest. The familiar nocturnal chorus of wildlife created a soothing background as we settled in. But in the early hours of the morning, an unsettling silence enveloped us, a stark contrast to the usual symphony of the night.

This eerie quietude was soon accompanied by a pungent, musky odor, so strong and unfamiliar that it filled the air with a heavy, almost tangible presence. It was unlike anything we had ever encountered, a scent that seemed to herald something primal and unknown. As we groped for our flashlights, a sudden, powerful shaking of our vehicle jolted us into a state of heightened alarm.

When we mustered the courage to look outside, our flashlights cut through the darkness to reveal an astonishing sight. There, in the dim light, stood a colossal creature, its figure casting a formidable shadow against the trees. It was the legendary Bigfoot, a being of myth, right before our eyes. Its massive frame was covered in coarse, matted fur, and its eyes, reflecting our flashlights, conveyed an almost human-like depth and intelligence.

Frozen in terror, we watched as this giant of the forest examined our vehicle with what seemed like a curious, albeit intimidating, demeanor. The sheer strength of the creature was undeniable as it rocked our SUV with ease, making us acutely aware of our vulnerability in its presence.

Driven by a primal urge to flee, we managed to start the SUV and hastily retreated from the scene. Glancing back, we saw the Bigfoot standing motionless, its gaze following us, a silent sentinel in the moonlit forest. This surreal encounter, lasting only minutes, felt like an eternity and left an indelible mark on our psyche.

In the aftermath, our perception of our cherished wilderness was irrevocably altered. The forest, once a haven of peace and adventure, now harbored a respectful fear, a reminder of the mysteries and unknown entities that dwell within its depths. Our story, once centered around the simplicity of nature and love, now included a chapter of awe and disbelief, a testament to the unexplained phenomena that lie beyond the realm of human understanding. This experience, though terrifying, also instilled in us a deeper reverence for the natural world and its hidden wonders, forever changing our narrative of camping and adventure.

2

SHADOW FIGURES

During my high school years, I was invited to a birthday celebration at my friend Emily's residence. She had recently relocated to a different city, so I was thrilled at the chance to reconnect. Emily was under house arrest at the time, which meant while her parents allowed a birthday gathering, an overnight stay was off the table. My own parents were reluctant to drive a great distance for a late-night pickup, but they understood how important this reunion was for me. Luckily, another friend of ours, Sarah, who lived about four miles from Emily's place and was also attending the party, agreed to let me stay with her. After getting her parents' approval, everything was set.

The long-awaited evening finally arrived, and my parents dropped me off, making me promise to call them once I reached Sarah's home, no matter the time. At the party, Emily, Sarah, and I, along with around a dozen other girls, enjoyed typical teenage games and a terrifying horror movie. The party wrapped up sharply at midnight, and Emily's parents, not as cordial as I remembered, ushered everyone out.

We were in Montana, in the heart of winter, with temperatures well below freezing. Without mobile phones, Sarah and I had to use the landline to inform her parents to pick us up, and we waited outside in the biting cold. Emily's house, situated at the end of a secluded lane, was surrounded by dense, shadowy forests, adding an eerie feel to our wait.

After about fifteen minutes, with everyone else gone and no sign of Sarah's parents, frustration and fear began to set in. Sarah then revealed that her parents hadn't answered the phone earlier. We were stuck. She suggested a trail through the forest that supposedly led directly to her backyard. Reluctant but without better options, we embarked on the daunting path through the dark woods.

Our journey was fraught with challenges. The trail abruptly ended, forcing us to navigate through dense trees and icy terrain. Sarah claimed familiarity with the path, but it was clear she was mistaken. We found another route, but it only led us deeper into the forest. The snow began to fall heavily, and our initial annoyance turned into genuine fear.

As we trudged on, a strange humming sound filled the air, intensifying into a piercing shriek that brought us to our knees. Growing up in Montana, I was no stranger to the woods, but nothing had prepared me for this. The noise eventually ceased, and we continued in silence, driven by a desperate desire to escape the forest.

Then, a bizarre, bright, diamond-shaped light appeared ahead. It seemed otherworldly, and as we approached, it suddenly vanished. The atmosphere around us changed inexplicably, heightening our sense of dread. Soon, we heard sounds of rapid movement around us, unlike anything natural.

In the most terrifying moment, we encountered a group of shadowy figures, about ten in total, eerily observing us. They appeared human but were composed of pure darkness. One, who seemed to be the leader, stood out with glowing green eyes and a distinct hat and coat, unaffected by the wind.

One by one, the shadow figures disappeared with loud pops, until only the leader remained. He pointed at us before vanishing himself, leaving us paralyzed with fear. The humming returned, transforming into a painful keening. As it subsided, we finally ran towards the nearby lights of civilization.

It felt like hours had passed, but upon reaching safety, it was only just past three in the morning. However, looking back at the woods, the mysterious light reappeared. We reached Sarah's house, her parents aghast at our ordeal. We explained it as getting lost in the woods, too shaken to share the full story.

In the following years, Sarah's health deteriorated inexplicably. She battled various ailments before succumbing to a rare disease at just 32. I've been left wondering why she suffered while I remained unaffected. Since that night, I've experienced sleep paralysis, often featuring the shadowy hat man, but nothing as intense as our encounter in the woods.

That's the essence of my harrowing experience. I continue to search for answers and hope to one day understand the mysteries we encountered in those Montana woods.

3

WHISPERS FROM THE FOREST

As a young boy, my family's yearly ritual was to journey from our home in southern Connecticut to a quaint town in the Green Mountains of Vermont. There, we rented a cabin that stood as a gateway to a world of natural wonders and youthful escapades. Those trips are etched in my memory as the pinnacle of my childhood joy. Our party always consisted of my mother, father, my two younger brothers, and me. Each summer, like clockwork, we'd secure our cabin. But first, let me paint a picture of the setting and dynamics before delving into the chilling encounter that forever changed my view of those woods.

These cabins, though isolated, were arranged akin to a summer camp. Multiple cabins dotted the landscape, and during our stays, the occupants of the neighboring cabins became our temporary community. I can't recall any unpleasant incidents with other vacationers; often, there were other children to mingle with. This tradition began with my parents' courtship and continued into my own childhood. In our area, there were five cabins, part of several such clusters spread throughout the forest. This was the 1980s, a time unmarred by the distractions of Wi-Fi or cell phones, leaving us kids to our own devices for entertainment. Our only rule was to return before nightfall. Other than that, we were free to roam. The summer of 1983, when I was thirteen, brought an experience so harrowing that it forever altered my perception of those idyllic vacations.

In that fateful summer, my brothers, aged eight and six, kept to their own amusements, while I sought out peers for exploration. Among the five cabins, only one other was occupied, a common scenario in early summer. As the season progressed, occupancy would peak, but I cherished the tranquility of the early days. One sweltering June day, I noticed a boy around my age staying in the neighboring cabin. His name was Alex, and he hailed from a town in Connecticut, the specifics of which now elude me. He was eleven and had a younger brother. After hours of hiking and fishing, we returned to find our families intertwined in a jovial evening of music, food, and laughter. That night, the summer routine felt enchantingly repetitive yet refreshingly new.

The cabin we rented had three bedrooms, with my parents opting for the largest to accommodate us comfortably. My brothers shared a room, and mine was adjacent. That night, after a quick shower, I retired to my room, which had bunk beds and a large window. Craving the night breeze, I left the window open and tried to sleep, my mind abuzz with excitement for the days ahead. Alex and I had bonded quickly, and the prospect of more adventures was thrilling. But as I drifted off, an eerie noise from outside jolted me awake. It was a heavy, prowling sound, too large to be any small animal. Despite my familiarity with the woods, I knew little of its larger inhabitants. Safety pamphlets provided cursory advice on encountering wild animals, but that was it.

Something about the noise instilled an instinctive dread in me. As I listened, it seemed as if a large creature was pacing outside my window. Peering into the darkness, I saw nothing. Dismissing it as a trick of my tired mind, I tried to sleep. However, curiosity soon won over, and I approached the window for a closer look. As I gazed out, two glowing red eyes met mine. A chilling growl followed, and I retreated to join my brothers in the living room, where I spent the rest of the night.

The next morning, eager to play with Alex again, I pushed aside the night's fear. That day passed without incident, and in the evening, Alex's family invited us over. We returned to our cabin late, and Alex stayed over. We slept in the top bunks, only to be awoken by a thunderous knocking. Approaching the door, a sense of dread washed over me. We heard my father's voice, but something was off. It sounded layered, almost inhuman. My father never called me 'son,' and he would have said 'us' instead of 'me.' We hesitated, sensing danger.

The knocking grew violent, and now my mother's voice joined, pleading in a similarly distorted tone. Terrified, we screamed for it to leave. Suddenly, the noise ceased, and we hesitantly approached the door. Then, we heard Alex's brother crying for help. As we stood frozen, the doorknob began to turn. We rushed to hold the door, but it was my real father who burst in, oblivious to our terror.

We explained our fear as a mistaken animal encounter, though internally, we knew it was something more sinister. Alex later confided he had also seen the red eyes and heard growls the previous night. For days, we avoided the woods, but eventually, our fear subsided, and we resumed our outdoor adventures.

The rest of the summer passed uneventfully, but the experience haunted me. Since then, I've felt a malevolent presence in the woods, as if something attached itself to me that summer. Despite this, my love for nature persists, and I've shared these tales with my children and grandchildren, cautioning them about the unseen dangers lurking in the wilderness. I lost touch with Alex but hope that, by some twist of fate, he might read this and reconnect, sharing if he too has been shadowed by that sinister force from our childhood.

4

AMONG THE TOMBSTONES

n the year 1994, when youthful arrogance led me to believe I knew all there was to know at the tender age of 16, I found myself in the midst of an eerie adventure that still haunts me. My name is Alex, a regular teenager in the small, sleepy town where everyone knew each other's business. My friends, Sarah, Mike, and Kevin, were the constants in my life – a group of misfits in our own right, bound by our shared sense of not fitting into the conventional cliques of high school. Sarah and Mike, a couple since a year, were part of our little quartet, and Kevin, quietly carrying a torch for Sarah, completed our circle.

Our town was the epitome of rural dullness – the kind of place where weekend entertainment was limited to field parties or finding creative ways to alleviate boredom. One such weekend, Sarah, whose parents frequently left her home alone, invited us over. With nothing else on the agenda, we eagerly accepted. We congregated at Sarah's house, situated at the far edge of town, a good 45-minute drive from where the rest of us lived. Mike, Kevin, and I, with our teenage minds, planned a night filled with horror flicks and drinking games, despite Sarah's half-hearted protests.

Upon arrival, we coaxed Sarah into unlocking her parents' liquor cabinet. The night progressed with each of us slipping further into a state of inebriated laughter, snacking intermittently in a vain attempt to counter the effects of the alcohol. Kevin, whose feelings for Sarah were an open secret, grew increasingly vocal about his disapproval of her relationship with Mike, especially under the influence of liquor.

The night wore on and our initial amusement with the movies and card games waned, leading to a restless search for a new thrill. Kevin, ever the instigator, proposed an impromptu visit to the old graveyard on the outskirts of town. The graveyard, a relic of the past, nestled within a dense thicket of woods, had long been abandoned. Local legends whispered of spirits and demonic entities haunting its grounds, and it had even been featured in a paranormal investigation on a popular streaming service. A medium who visited the site had proclaimed the presence of a malevolent force, something akin to the devil itself, claiming it trapped souls within its confines.

In our half-drunken state, this tale only added a tinge of excitement to the idea. We didn't genuinely believe we'd capture a ghost on Kevin's old Polaroid, but the bragging rights of having ventured there past midnight seemed appealing. We failed to heed the warnings from the show, unaware that we were stepping into a realm of darkness and potential danger.

Arriving at the cemetery, we were greeted by the remnants of previous visitors – the usual litter left behind by teenagers seeking their own thrill. The grave-yard's history stretched back to the 1600s, its past mired in tragedy and sorrow. We had grown up hearing stories of its haunted paths, but they were just that – stories, or so we thought.

As we wandered, Sarah and Mike split off, seeking some privacy, leaving Kevin and me to explore. Kevin's frustration with their relationship bubbled over, and in a moment of thoughtless rebellion, we both ended up relieving ourselves on a weathered tombstone. This act, disrespectful and foolish, would later come back to haunt us in ways we couldn't imagine.

Not long after, a blood-curdling scream echoed through the graveyard. It was Sarah and Mike. Panic set in, and Kevin and I rushed toward the sound. A heavy sense of being watched enveloped us, and the air grew thick with an unspoken fear. We found Sarah and Mike in a state of terror. Sarah was curled up on the ground, shaking, while Mike stood beside her, anger and fear etched on his face. Before we could ask what happened, our attention was diverted to something behind us – a colossal shadowy figure, standing ominously a short distance away.

This entity was unlike anything we had ever seen – it loomed over us, at least ten feet tall, with an aura of sheer malevolence. In a blind panic, we all ran back to the car, the entity seemingly in pursuit. Sarah struggled to start the car, her hands trembling as the rest of us yelled in terror. The car shook violently as if hit by an immense force, leaving us paralyzed with fear.

When the car finally roared to life, Sarah drove like a person possessed, eager to escape the nightmare we had unwittingly stumbled into. Back at her house, we were too shaken to even consider stepping out of the car, fearing that the entity had followed us. Eventually, we gathered the courage to go inside, but the terror of the night clung to us like a cold shroud.

We debated whether to look at the photos we had taken. Curiosity overcame our fear, and we sifted through the Polaroids. The images were chilling – the first few were innocuous, but then we saw it: a pair of glowing red eyes near the gravestone we had desecrated. In another photo, a human-sized shadow figure loomed behind Sarah and Mike. The most terrifying image was of the giant shadow entity, surrounded by smaller, similar beings, all exuding an air of malevolence.

The experience left us deeply shaken. We agreed to burn the photos, hoping to sever any ties to that horrifying night. We never spoke of it at school, wary of what might happen if the story spread. The incident changed us – I began to avoid graveyards and developed a distaste for horror. Sarah, Mike, and I remained in touch, but Kevin moved away not long after, and we lost contact.

Years later, as I reflect on that night, I'm still plagued by questions. What were those entities? Demons, ghosts, or something else entirely? I may never know, and perhaps it's for the best. But the fear remains, a constant reminder of the night we faced the shadows among the tombstones. Thank you for letting me share this unnerving chapter of my life.

5

INTERDIMENSIONAL HELL

eginning this narrative, I must confess that the natural world and I were always at odds. Raised in a bustling, medium-sized urban area, the very concept of camping was as foreign to me as a distant planet. My entire family – encompassing parents, grandparents, cousins, and siblings – never embraced the outdoors. We were urbanites through and through, content with our city lives. So, it might be surprising to learn that my first and most terrifying encounter with the unknown happened in the heart of nature at the age of thirty-nine. This story unfolds at a time when I was grappling with a tumultuous divorce and the recent loss of my father. In an attempt to redis-cover myself and find solace, I embarked on a spiritual journey. This path, which seemed unrelated at first, was what ultimately led me to the wilderness.

The catalyst for this adventure was a session with my spiritual guide, Leo. He had a serene presence and an air of knowing that often put me at ease. During one of our sessions, he foretold that I was on the cusp of discovering my true purpose on this earth. He urged me to be vigilant for signs and symbols in the coming week. Remarkably, I kept encountering references to a specific region several states away. These signs appeared in various forms – in television commercials, movies, and even in my dreams. After discussing these occurrences with Leo, we concluded that it was essential for me to reconnect with nature. Our destination was decided, but I refrained from naming it explicitly here, hoping to shield others from the horrors I encountered.

In preparation for this journey, I requested and received a two-week leave from work. I delved into exhaustive research about the chosen site and the basics of camping. Leo, a seasoned nature lover, was to accompany me. He had learned of a mystical and secluded spot from one of his clients, which he felt was perfect for our spiritual expedition. The site turned out to be far more remote than I had imagined, but I placed my trust in Leo's guidance. We embarked on a lengthy seven-hour drive, followed by a strenuous hike to reach our intended campsite. Our plan was to completely disconnect from our regular lives, leaving behind our phones and worldly worries in the car.

Upon reaching the site, we worked together to set up our temporary home amidst the trees. The process was smoother than anticipated, and soon we found ourselves settling into the tranquility of the forest. We spent the evening reading, discussing, and immersing ourselves in the peaceful sounds of the woods. However, this tranquility was short-lived. That night, I was jolted awake by a disturbing, pig-like grunting sound, which was accompanied by unnervingly human-like heavy breathing. Filled with fear and uncertainty, Leo and I remained as still as possible, trying to convince ourselves it was just a forest animal. Despite our fears, we somehow managed to fall back asleep, even as the unsettling sounds seemed to draw nearer to our tent.

The following morning, we inspected our campsite, finding everything in its place. We decided to proceed with our planned solo hikes. I chose a trail that appeared relatively straightforward at the outset. As I progressed, however, I was startled by a distant yet simultaneously close humming sound. It disoriented me, causing dizziness and confusion. Alarmed, I decided to head back towards the campsite. But as I retraced my steps, the trail seemed unfamiliar, marked by noticeable features I had not observed earlier.

The forest had become eerily silent. The absence of animal sounds, the stillness of the trees despite the visible movement of their branches – the silence was oppressive. My heart raced as I noticed a fleeting black shape near a large tree. Despite my inner alarms, curiosity compelled me to investigate. I kept seeing and following these enigmatic movements, leading me further away from the path. Periodically, I would snap back to reality, realizing the danger of my situation, but each time, an inexplicable urge pushed me to continue my pursuit.

As night began to fall, my sense of time became distorted. My watch had stopped working, and the wind started howling violently around me. Strangely, I found myself unable to leave a small area, as if confined by an invisible barrier. In the darkness, intensified by pouring rain, I observed pale, grotesque creatures moving on all fours outside the barrier. Their joints popped disturbingly with each movement, and their teeth were a nightmarish array of yellow and green. Their mocking screams and attempts to breach the barrier filled me with dread.

Exhausted and terrified, I eventually lost consciousness, only to awaken during an airlift rescue with Leo by my side. Once safe in the hospital, I recounted the entire ordeal to him. Although initially skeptical, Leo listened intently. I remembered being fed strange meat by smaller beings, equally terrifying but seemingly protective against the larger creatures.

Leo and I hypothesized that I had inadvertently

stumbled into an interdimensional portal. Perhaps I had been marked or chosen by these entities the previous night. Despite undergoing therapy and engaging in continuous spiritual cleansing with Leo, the experience left deep scars. I remain haunted by the memories, plagued by nightmares and an enduring fear of darkness. I now stick to the safety of my urban environment, constantly wondering if these entities might one day return.

This encounter has profoundly changed me. The everyday sights and sounds of the city provide a semblance of normalcy, but there's always a part of me that remains vigilant, watchful for any signs of their return. My once mundane existence has been irrevocably altered by this brush with the unknown, leaving me to question the very nature of reality and our place within it. The experience, while terrifying, has also opened my eyes to the vast and mysterious possibilities that lie beyond our understanding. As I continue my journey of healing and discovery, I hold onto the hope that the knowledge gained from this harrowing adventure will one day lead to a deeper understanding of the world beyond our own.

6

THEY CAME WITH THE WIND

rowing up, my life was far from typical. Raised by a teenage mother, my father was a stranger to me. Our bond was more like close friends than the traditional mother-son dynamic. It was just the two of us; I was her only child. When this eerie tale unfolded, I was twelve, and my mom was tirelessly working to provide for us. She had a fascination with mystical and spiritual elements. Most of my early years were spent accompanying her to various occult shops and vintage stores, scouring for peculiar artifacts to stock her newly opened boutique. My grandmother had generously funded the initial rental for her shop, agreeing to cover the first few months.

My mother's small business started gaining traction, and we were finally able to afford a place of our own. Mom was sociable and easily made friends with many of her customers. One of them, a lady named Sarah, became a close confidante. Sarah, like my mom, was unmarried and shared her passion for the metaphysical. They grew inseparable, and Sarah eventually began working in the shop. I had a deep affection for her, and even now, a decade later, our bond remains strong.

However, I sometimes wonder if opening that store was the beginning of our misfortunes. My mother, initially intrigued by spiritual healing and crystal energies, was nowhere near as entrenched in these practices as Sarah. They dabbled in it more as a hobby, albeit an obsessive one. One night, something changed. Sarah visited, and after our usual routine of horror films and their late-night talks, the next day brought a peculiar excitement. Sarah had introduced us to divining rods.

Neither my mother nor I knew much about these rods, but their potential intrigued us. Despite numerous online warnings about their use, we were too excited to heed them. We decided to explore the woods behind our house with the rods. It was a spontaneous decision, made without waiting for Sarah, who had a prior engagement that evening.

The woods were dense and foreboding. Armed with flashlights and the rods, we ventured deep into the unknown. A sense of fear overwhelmed us at a particular spot in the woods, but we brushed it aside and began using the rods. They pointed us deeper into the forest, guiding us through an inexplicable journey.

As we prepared to head back, my mother's behavior with the rods suddenly changed. They jerked violently, directing us to a massive, dark shape emitting eerie noises. Terrified, we ran back to our house, chased by this shadowy entity. It assaulted our back door with ferocious bangs, growling and groaning menacingly.

The disturbances didn't end that night. For the next four years, our home was plagued by incessant banging, window tapping, and inhuman noises. Despite consulting various psychics and spiritual experts, the haunting persisted. Sarah introduced us to a physical medium who ultimately convinced my mother to move.

Tragically, my mother's life was cut short at thirty-two, a victim of a violent crime. Sarah believes the entity followed us, contributing to the tragedy. Despite my efforts, the true nature of that night's entity remains a mystery. Some speculate the divining rods alerted us to its presence, sparing us from a worse fate.

Haunted by unanswered questions and unresolved fears, I've chosen to move forward with my life. This account is my final attempt to share and perhaps exorcise these haunting memories. Thank you for allowing me to unload this burden. Perhaps in the future, I might delve into other experiences linked to that fateful encounter.

7

AN UNFORGETTABLE WILDERNESS EXPERIENCE

As a woman in my mid-sixties, I often find myself reflecting on the various chapters of my life. I'm not one to easily label myself as "elderly," but I've certainly accumulated a wealth of experiences. One such experience, which remains vivid in my memory, occurred during a camping expedition with my local community group.

My early life was quite traditional for its time. Married young and a mother shortly thereafter, I found my identity largely intertwined with that of my family. My husband, though not abusive, was a dominant presence, and my life revolved around his needs and preferences. It wasn't until his untimely passing from a sudden stroke a couple of years ago that I began exploring my own interests—one of which was camping, a pastime he never enjoyed.

Eager to embark on new adventures, I was thrilled when my community group announced a spiritual retreat combined with a camping trip for individuals over sixty. It was scheduled for a long weekend in a remote region of Montana, known for its sprawling meadows and thick forests. I had been an active member of this group for several years, but it was only after my husband's death that I began forming deeper bonds with its members. Among them was my dear friend Elizabeth, who became my closest confidante and encouraged me to embrace life's possibilities.

Our journey took us deep into the heart of nature, away from the bustle of city life. I was both excited and slightly apprehensive, having led a sheltered life. Elizabeth's bold and adventurous spirit complemented my more reserved nature, helping me break free from the shell I had built around myself.

We arrived at the campsite in the early afternoon, setting up our tents in pairs. While I knew everyone in the group by name, I looked forward to deepening these acquaintances. The first evening was magical—sharing stories around the campfire, a sense of community, and the thrill of my first night in the wilderness.

However, the serenity of the night was soon shattered. A couple of hours into my sleep, I was jolted awake by unsettling noises outside my tent. The sounds were unlike anything I'd heard before—a bizarre blend of animalistic growls and what seemed eerily human. Elizabeth and I, tents pitched side by side, quickly huddled together, trying to make sense of the chilling scene unfolding before us.

Peering out, we saw numerous pairs of eyes— glowing red, green, and yellow—fixated on us. The fear was palpable as we debated whether to alert our group leader, Sarah. Ultimately, we decided to stay put and pray for safety.

The prayers seemed to have an effect, as the strange creatures retreated after emitting agonizing shrieks. The next morning, the atmosphere was tense. Everyone, including Sarah, had experienced the same terror. A sense of unity emerged from our shared fear and the belief that our collective prayers had somehow protected us.

The experience took a darker turn on our departure. Upon reaching the nearby visitor center, we were met with police activity. Sarah discovered that a nearby camp of young people had been viciously attacked the night of our arrival, their tents torn apart by something unidentifiable. This revelation sent chills down our spines. Had our prayers saved us from a similar fate?

In the aftermath, I found myself pondering the nature of our encounter. I delved into local legends and folklore, uncovering tales of creatures akin to werewolves in the region. These explorations opened my eyes to mysteries beyond human understanding.

Our group never embarked on another overnight retreat, opting instead for day trips. The experience left an indelible mark on us all, challenging our beliefs and understanding of the world. For me, it was a stark reminder of the vast and mysterious forces that exist just beyond the veil of our everyday reality.

8

MYSTERIES OF THE FOREST GROVE

Throughout my life, I've encountered a myriad of unexplainable events. My skepticism has long since faded, replaced by a firm belief in the extraordinary. Countless stories and videos have solidified my conviction that these phenomena are genuine. This belief stems from an unforgettable incident that occurred when I was fourteen. In recent years, the enigma of people vanishing in forests, often under the gaze of onlookers, has captured public attention. My own experience, however, lends me a unique perspective on these disappearances.

As a child growing up in the bustling metropolis of Harbour City, my playground was the urban landscape. My circle of friends, including my closest pal, Danny, and I, rarely ventured beyond our familiar streets. Our world was small, and technology like the internet or smartphones was yet to reshape our lives. Our childhood games were simple, played under the watchful eye of streetlights and parental boundaries.

The mystery of these forest disappearances resonates with me. I believe a multitude of factors contributes to these tragic losses. Let me share my story, which might shed light on these dark, wooded enigmas.

Danny's fourteenth birthday was the catalyst for our unforgettable adventure. He decided to celebrate at "the grove," a forested area two hours from Harbour City. This spot was our occasional escape to what we naively called "the great outdoors." His birthday fell on a Friday, and his parents planned a lakeside barbecue for Danny, myself, and a few other neighborhood boys.

On the day of our departure, we were brimming with excitement. The grove was a haven for us - a landscape of dense forests surrounding a serene lake, complete with picnic tables, barbecues, and fire pits. The freedom to explore these woods was a thrilling prospect.

After enjoying a swim and a hearty lunch, Danny and I decided to venture into the woods, a decision that would soon lead to the most bizarre experience of my life. We were fearless city boys, unaware of the dangers that lay hidden in the natural world.

We set off into the forest around noon, our spirits high. We planned to play a game of hide and seek, unaware of how drastically our day was about to change. As I ran to hide, the world around me transformed in the blink of an eye. The bright day turned to dusk, the air grew thick, and I found myself in an environment that resembled a rainforest more than the familiar woods of the grove.

Panic set in as I realized I was lost in an alien landscape. The vegetation was dense and unfamiliar, and the atmosphere was heavy with an eerie sense of being watched. Desperately, I called out for Danny, but there was no response. All I could see was a strange, gray haze behind me, and a clear path lay ahead.

As I walked, the feeling of being pursued grew stronger. I was certain that something was stalking me through this unfamiliar terrain. The path ahead grew darker, and the gray haze behind me seemed to consume the trail I had just walked. It was a surreal and terrifying experience.

Suddenly, a voice called out, "Come here!" followed by the sensation of a claw gripping my shoulder. I screamed, and in an instant, everything reverted to normal. I was back in the familiar woods, with Danny's voice counting in the distance. I was overcome with relief but also confusion and fear.

I hurried back to Danny, my mind racing with the bizarre and frightening events I had just experienced. We decided to return to our families and explain what had happened. However, as we walked back, doubt crept in. Would anyone believe my incredible story?

My mother immediately sensed something was amiss when we reached the lake. Despite my jumbled explanation, the adults concluded that someone had attempted to abduct me. The police were called, and a report was filed. The experience left me shaken, and I spent the following weeks under my mother's watchful eye.

Since that day, I have been haunted by vivid nightmares of the creature I encountered. In these dreams, I see a massive, fanged beast with haunting green eyes. The experience at the grove has led me to believe in the existence of interdimensional portals. I am convinced that what I encountered was not of this world.

The incident has left me with a deep aversion to forests. The nightmares continue to plague me, suggesting that the creature, whatever it may be, still yearns for me. The terror of that day remains etched in my memory, a stark reminder of the mysteries that lurk in the depths of the woods. I have vowed never to venture into those, or any other, forests again.

9

ENCOUNTER WITH THE UNKNOWN

n the secluded woodlands of northern Maine, my childhood was filled with adventures. Our house, nestled near an ancient cemetery, was surrounded by dense forests, a natural playground for us. The woods, teeming with wildlife, and the old cemetery became our favorite haunts. Our parents, convinced of the safety of these woods, rarely objected to our explorations.

These forests were crisscrossed by streams that had once been vital for trade in the region, with goods transported on rafts. Our adventures in these woods were less structured than our Boy Scout excursions or family hunting trips, but no less exciting. I was twelve during the incident that has stayed with me throughout my life.

Local teenagers often partied in these woods, leaving behind a trail of debris. It was during one of our "treasure hunts" that my friend Peter and I decided to spend an evening fishing after dusk, a decision that would lead to an unforgettable encounter.

That night, after my parents left for a movie with my younger brother, Peter and I headed to our secret fishing spot. The woods felt eerily silent, a phenomenon we referred to as "dead air". It was an unsettling stillness that I now understand was far from normal.

As we settled down to fish, a sense of unease gripped us. We couldn't pinpoint the cause, but the atmosphere was distinctly different. Suddenly, I had the unnerving feeling of being watched, a sentiment Peter shared. Our conversation ceased as we listened intently, but only the sound of the nearby stream and rustling leaves reached our ears.

Then, a distant, unearthly scream shattered the quiet. Peter dropped his fishing rod in shock, and I was ready to flee, but he held me back, whispering for silence. The scream was unlike any animal cry we knew – and it didn't sound human either. When the scream repeated, closer this time, we realized something was profoundly wrong.

A guttural moan from a nearby thicket made our hearts race. Peter shone his flashlight towards the sound, revealing a towering figure, at least eight feet tall, with a broad, imposing stance. Covered in dark, matted fur, it stood half-hidden behind a tree, as if uncertain whether to conceal itself or come into the open.

As it stepped forward, the moonlight revealed its immense size and a strangely human-like gaze. Fear rooted us to the spot, but I whispered to Peter to back away slowly. The creature advanced with another scream, sending Peter running back towards the house. I hesitated, but when the creature made another move, I followed in panic.

We reached the edge of the woods, breathless and terrified. Peter was visibly shaken, and I urged him to hurry as the creature's screams echoed behind us. Safely home, we confessed everything to my parents upon their return. They were concerned, but not angry, and promised to investigate the next morning.

However, when we returned to the spot with my father, all our gear was gone. We found no trace of our visitor from the previous night. The experience left me with a deep sense of curiosity and respect for the unknown creatures that might inhabit our forests.

Since then, I've had several encounters, each unique but marked by the same eerie scream and cautious curiosity. I've never found physical evidence like footprints, but the memories of those glowing eyes and the feeling of being observed have stayed with me.

I believe these creatures, which I suspect to be a form of Bigfoot, possess a sense of humanity in their eyes, a kind of silent communication that transcends our under-standing. Their screams, though terrifying, seem more a display of presence than a threat.

As I continue to explore these woods, I plan to docu-ment each encounter, hoping to unravel more about these fascinating beings. Each meeting teaches me some-thing new, and I can't help but feel a deep, intuitive connection with these mysterious guardians of the forest. Thank you for allowing me to share my story.

10

THE ENIGMA

Back in my high school days, I had a relationship with a girl named Clara. We lived in the same neighborhood, and she was a year junior to me. Clara was genuinely kind-hearted, and our relationship, typical of high school, was brief yet memorable. After a few months, we went our separate ways. Despite this, we managed to maintain a friendly connection for some time before eventually losing touch. Years later, Clara reconnected with me on social media, and I was eager to accept her friend request. I had a network of high school friends on my social media, including Clara, and I occasionally met some of them in person.

Clara reached out to me with an urgent tone in her message. She had seen a post about my upcoming trip, a solo journey across the country to Colorado, specifically to the mysterious Whispering Pines. My choice of Whispering Pines stemmed from a deep-rooted fascination with the mystical and unexplained. The plan was to drive from my home in Virginia, immersing myself for a week in the wilderness, partly as a quest for spiritual clarity. At this point in my life, I was grappling with personal challenges, and I had recently discovered a YouTube channel that delved into mindfulness, meditation, and the power of positive thinking. Although I was a novice in mountain hiking and camping, I was familiar with the woods around my home, but they lacked the dense, enigmatic aura of Whispering Pines. I felt drawn to this journey, believing it could be transformative. I hoped not only to find inner peace but also to possibly encounter something extraordinary, like a mystical being or a gateway to another realm.

Emily's excitement, however, wasn't about my spiritual journey. She was eager to share her own experience at Whispering Pines, which she and her friends had visited for a ten-day camping trip the previous year. She narrated a story so profound and unusual that it vastly contrasted with my uneventful experience. Emily gave me her blessing to share her tale, and here it is, retold in my words.

Emily and her companions had chosen Whispering Pines for its seclusion and the allure of the unknown. Their initial days were calm, but by the third day, a peculiar sense of being observed crept upon them. They discussed it but attributed it to the natural paranoia of being in an unfamiliar, isolated environment. On their third night, as they shared scary stories around the campfire, their conversation circled back to this uneasy feeling of an unseen presence. Although they considered it might be a wild animal, the continuous snapping of branches in the distance kept them on edge. They tried to dismiss their fears, eventually turning their talk to lighter subjects before retiring to their separate tents.

The sensation of being watched lingered over the next few days, heightening their anxiety. It wasn't until the seventh day that their unease turned to genuine fear. During a hike, one friend, feeling exhausted, decided to turn back, leaving them in a quandary. They had agreed not to split up, but now one of them would have to be alone either way. The decision was made for Emily to continue the hike solo, while the others returned to camp. They agreed on a two-hour window for Emily's return, after which they would seek help.

As Emily ventured alone, the feeling of being followed intensified. Hearing branches crack and an eerie whistling, she feared a lurking predator, possibly human. Realizing she didn't have bear spray, her anxiety escalated. The whistling, initially sounding human-like, soon morphed into something more unsettling.

Determined to return to camp, Emily tried to ignore the continuous whistling, which now transformed into a purring noise. This confused her, as it was unlike any known wildlife behavior. Approaching the camp, the purring suddenly escalated into a shriek. Overcoming her initial hesitation, Emily turned to face the source of the noise and encountered a towering, ten-foot-tall creature covered in dark fur. Despite its intimidating appearance and foul odor, Emily felt a strange sense of calm. The creature, which appeared shy and curious, hid behind a tree, almost as if playing a game. Emily felt an inexplicable connection and wanted to approach it, but was startled by a loud, inhuman shriek and a voice in her head urging her to run.

She rushed back to camp, where her friends were already terrified by the strange noises. Despite their fear, Emily convinced them to stay for the remainder of the trip. She secretly hoped to encounter the creature again, feeling a magical connection to it. Emily's experience left her believing she had met a Bigfoot-like creature with a mystical aura.

As for my trip to Whispering Pines, I had no such encounters. I am both relieved and intrigued by Emily's story. We believe there might be a sentient creature in Whispering Pines, possibly seeking friendship or displaying harmless curiosity. Emily and I plan to return to Whispering Pines soon, hoping to uncover more about this mysterious creature. The experience has left us both fascinated and eager to explore the unknown.

The rest of my trip passed in a blur of introspection and natural beauty. I hiked through dense forests, meditated under the open sky, and felt a deep connection with the earth. The tranquility of Whispering Pines was a stark contrast to the dramatic encounter Emily described. Her story lingered in my mind, a fascinating puzzle amidst the serene backdrop.

As I prepared to leave Whispering Pines, I felt a mix of emotions. The peace and clarity I found were profound, yet Emily's tale added a layer of mystery to the place. It made me wonder about the unseen forces of nature and the potential for extraordinary encounters in the wilderness.

In the following months, Emily and I planned our trip meticulously. We researched the area, gathered supplies, and prepared ourselves for any possibility. Our excitement was palpable, fueled by the anticipation of discovering the unknown. We wondered if we would encounter the creature Emily had seen, or if new mysteries awaited us.

As we set out on our journey back to Whispering Pines, our spirits were high. The road ahead promised adventure, discovery, and perhaps a deeper understanding of the mysteries that nature holds. Whispering Pines awaited us, its secrets veiled in the shadows of the towering trees and the whispers of the wind. Our adventure was just beginning.

PUBLISHER'S EXCERPT 1

FEAR IN THE FOREST: VOLUME 1

ANGRY SPIRITS FROM THE WOODS

I inherited a cabin that belonged to my grandparents when I was twenty eight years old. It was a shock as they both died tragically, suddenly and together but also because no one knew they even owned a cabin. We are from the northeastern part of the United States and that's where most of my family was born and raised and where most of them still reside to this day. So, it was shocking when the will was read and I was told I had inherited a large chunk of money and a rustic, old cabin in the middle of the woods in Colorado. I was excited and couldn't have been more pleased. I could certainly use the money at the time even though I was unmarried and didn't have any kids yet. It afforded me the opportunity to be able to do some things I had always wanted to do but that I had been putting off in the rat race that is the corporate world where I worked. I broke the lease on my tiny apartment in the city, bought myself an old and used camper-van, stuffed it full of my belongings and headed out to Colorado within a week of inheriting the cabin. I had a job where I mainly worked from home but I took a few weeks off anyway because I wanted to be able to settle in and have some peace and quiet to myself. I was always very close with my grandparents, being the only grandchild, and though I was devastated at the loss, I felt so grateful to them for looking out for me the way that they had. My parents weren't happy about my moving to Colorado on what they called "a whim" but I knew it was the right thing for me to do at that time. Personally I just think they were jealous I was left a lot more than they were but I never would have said that to their faces. I promised my mother that as soon as I got settled in I would let her know and then if they wanted to they could come and check out the cabin. She settled for that much and I left without ever planning on looking back.

I had no idea how far out into the sticks the cabin was. I figured it would be fairly isolated given how my grandparents always valued their privacy but I got quite a shock when I spent a half hour's time driving on three separate, country, back roads, each! It was literally in the middle of nowhere and in the middle of the woods. I was definitely not used to being out in the country and had never been camping, hunting, hiking or anything like that my entire life. I had always wanted to do those things and I figured there was no time like the present. What I hadn't been told was that the cabin they owned was a part of an old summer camp that shut down in the sixties and they sold off the cabins one by one to the highest bidders. To me that was crazy but it ended up being pretty cool. I had neighbors, somewhere around in between all the trees and other woods and there was a huge lake in the compound as well. I didn't see any other cabins on the drive into the place and I hadn't even seen a gas station in the last twenty miles or so but I knew there had to have been other people there, especially at that time of year. It was the end of fall and winter was just starting to rear its ugly head. I knew it snowed a lot in Colorado but that wasn't anything I was used to, or so I thought, having lived in a big city on the northeastern seaboard my whole life. I had no clue what I was in for, and not only with the weather either. It didn't take long for me to get my first dose of the terrifying and the supernatural things that came from those woods and had, somehow and at some point, become a part of that cabin and everything around it.

I had to bring in some professionals to do small jobs on various parts of the building and land but it was all very minor things and initial inspections, stuff like that. They were all local companies I had found in the yellow pages. It was odd though that when I would answer the door they would always take a step back and every single one of them refused my offer to come inside and warm up for a minute before or after doing what they needed to do. Finally one of them, a woman who had to come in to make sure all of my wires and things were up to date, flat out said, "There's no way I'm going in there so please be honest and answer the questions I'm about to ask you."

I thought it was kind of rude and she blatantly explained that my cabin was said to be haunted and all types of crazy things had been seen and heard coming from there, mainly at night throughout the course of all the years since the camp closed down. While she refused to get into any more detail she said that a few years back my grandparents had to be called out there because there were people performing rituals in there and someone had called the police and she also claimed that the tragedies there were unnatural and occurred way more than what would be considered a normal amount, starting all the way back when it was still a summer camp. She told me it was a literal portal to hell because it had been built on top of one. I was in shock and thought she was crazy. I answered her questions and couldn't have been more pleased when she was finally off my porch.

At first I noticed a lot of little, weird things happening in the cabin but nothing that alarmed me or made me feel unsafe or like I was living on top of a portal to hell. The one thing was the constant and almost obsessive banging that would happen every single night when I would lay down for bed. I would lay down and listen to my music fairly loudly on the radio because it helped me to unwind and fall asleep faster. I listened to classical music before bed but it seemed like every single time I would turn it on, there would be a strange banging sound like someone was stomping up and down on the floor right next to me but there was no one there. I heard it a lot when I was in my bedroom specifically but it was never as bad as when I was playing my music before bed. I'm gonna make a long story short here but one thing aside from the banging was a feeling like I was always being watched, not just inside of the house but outside as well. It felt like the woods had taken on a life of their own and something within them was always watching me. It was eerie and made spending time on the back deck and enjoying the beautiful view not even worth it anymore. I didn't go out there much after the first month.

Finally the time came when my parents were insisting they wanted to come and visit and so they did. It was right before the first major snowfall of the season and they got to my house just in time to end up snowed in with me. We had a good time but my mother came in one day and asked me if I had met the old woman who used to live here. I asked her what she was talking about and she said she had been on the back deck smoking a cigarette when a little old lady came up and asked her how she likes the place. My mother explained to her that she loved it and was thinking about buying one of them in the area herself. The old woman told her that she used to live in my cabin but now she lived somewhere else. The woman pointed in the direction to the back of the house and into the woods. That wasn't too worrisome or unbelievable because the other cabins were located all within the woods and throughout the area. It was very rugged and also very massive so I knew I hadn't seen all of the cabins yet despite having been there for a little over a month. The activity in the cabin was getting bad and my parents and I noticed shadow entities in the corners and they also seemed to be standing at the foot of the beds in the middle of the night but it was all chalked up to us possibly seeing things. When it came to the things that would be there one minute and gone the next like keys, the remote or even a hairbrush, we convinced ourselves that we had simply been mistaken about where we had left those items in the first place. Then one night, everything changed.

I was upstairs in my room, listening to my classical music and getting ready for bed when the banging started. There was an empty bedroom in the room below me where I had one bed and the rest of my boxes I still had to unpack. Across from that room, on the ground floor was the guest room where my parents were staying. The banging was so loud I went downstairs and asked my parents if they could hear it and they said they thought it was coming from the room across from theirs and they had been hearing it every night like I had. I think up until that point none of us wanted to accept that maybe the place was haunted. We all went into the spare room to look and see if we could figure it out but there was nothing there. As we all turned to leave something caught my eye in the mirror and I kid you not I screamed like a little girl. There, sitting on the bed directly across from the mirror was a little old lady with blazing red eyes. She had a broom in her hand and as she looked at me and smiled a terrifying and evil grin, she started slamming the broom handle into the ceiling above her. That was what the banging had been the whole time. Suddenly, as both my parents turned to look, the lady could be seen on the bed and she got up and angrily stormed towards us. She yelled in a demonic voice for us to get the hell out of her house. I didn't know what else to do so we ran from the room and I slammed the door in her face. We were in such a panic we ran out the back door and were on the deck. It was snowing like crazy.

There were footprints in the snow leading from my back deck, down the few stairs and into the woods. I thought someone had broken in and my rational mind said the old lady was in on it. When my mother told me it was the same old woman she had seen that had said she used to live there, I became furious and thought my hillbilly neighbors were trying to rob me. I grabbed my jacket and ran into the woods to follow the footprints. It was dark outside at that time but I had brought a flashlight, thank God for my mother who had thought ahead. I shined it everywhere but didn't see anything around me but I knew someone was watching me the whole time. I yelled for whoever it was to show themselves and called them a coward and some other choice and not so nice words. Suddenly, the footprints stopped at the lake. I looked up but there was no one there and other than my own there were no footprints anywhere. That's when

I looked up and saw shadow beings with glowing red eyes all around me, coming out from behind the trees. They started walking towards me and in my terror I could do nothing but scream. They all looked startled for a minute and I thought for a second it was me who had somehow been able to intimidate them. They all turned their heads at the same time towards the lake, which was frozen over and snow covered. There, directly in the middle of the lake, there was a huge, black figure. It was blacker than the darkness of the night and looked like it was wearing a cloak or hood of some kind. It was at least thirteen feet tall and carried a scythe. It looked almost like the comic book and horror movie images of Death itself. And it was coming right towards me.

As the regular sized shadow beings closed in on me I took off running. I ran as fast as I could back to my house but on the way the old lady came out from behind a tree. She was almost snarling, her eyes blazing. She shook her broom at me and told me, again in the demonic voice, to get out of her house. I didn't stop and ran right into her, knocking her down into the snow in the process. She let out an ear piercing howl behind me and when I turned around she was gone. There was a huge mark in the snow though where she had fallen on the ground. I kept running but right before I got to my house, I saw that the giant shadow/Death being was standing on the stairs to the back porch. It was perfectly still and its cloak wasn't blowing in the breeze or anything. It also seemed to be completely unaffected by the snow as it remained pristine and untouched by the stuff. It pulled a pocket watch or something similar out of its pocket, looked at it, and then looked back at me. It started to walk towards me and all I could think to do was pray. I prayed fervently like I had never prayed before. When I opened my eyes it was gone but I could still feel a presence watching me from the woods. I ran inside and eventually I calmed down enough to tell my parents what happened. They believed me but there wasn't anywhere we could go. We were snowed in, in a cabin in the middle of nowhere and there was no way out. There was a state of emergency outside and in most of the state at the time so only emergency vehicles were allowed to be on the roads for any reason. We were stuck there, at least for a little while.

The activity got worse and worse as each day passed and I could write a book about everything terrifying that went on in that place. My parents and I all slept together in the living room and eventually we came to discuss why my grandparents had given me the cabin and none of us could understand it. Once the snow cleared my parents went home and begged me to go with them. I couldn't though because I loved the cabin itself and the land around it too much. I called in some specialists who deal with the paranormal and one of them was a medicine woman from a Native tribe in the area. She told me I had angered the Great Spirit in the woods and that he felt like he and I were at war. Therefore he was attacking me and sending in all of the resources available to him. She said that if I earnestly apologized and gave a peace offering, that he MIGHT allow me to stay and live there in peace. I thought it was all mumbo jumbo and thought that I was dealing with something definitely evil and from hell itself. However, I was willing to try anything at that point and so I did what she told me to do. I bought some tobacco and a small bottle of liquor and went out to the edge of the woods. I apologized with my arms out to what or whoever the Great Spirit was and suddenly, for the first time since I had been there I felt at peace. I even felt something touch my hand as though it were shaking it. The "war" was over, apparently.

I bring gifts to the Spirit at the start of every season and I still live in the cabin. I had to learn to live with the shadow beings but the huge one I thought was death hasn't shown up again since I made peace with the entity in the woods. They torment me sometimes but it's always in waves and then for a few months it'll all be quiet. I had to bring in a medium to get rid of the old lady and the rest is, as they say, history. I've contemplated just selling the place but it has a hold on me and I'm somewhat attached to it now. Also, I don't want anyone else to have to go through what I went through with the Spirit in the woods or that I still go through with the shadow beings. Since no one knows what they are or where they come from, there's really no getting rid of them. There are several documented cases where they're said to have killed people but I keep close to my faith and that's all I can do. Thanks for letting me share.

———

FEAR IN THE FOREST: VOLUME 1

PUBLISHER'S EXCERPT 2

ENCOUNTERS BIGFOOT: VOLUME 1

INDIANA ENCOUNTER

Back in August of 1985, during the tranquil evening hours around twilight, an extraordinary event unfolded while my brothers and I were strolling along the railroad tracks behind our house, heading towards Fort Wayne.

Now, Fort Wayne may seem like an unlikely place for a bigfoot sighting, but regardless, I'm here to recount what we witnessed that day.

As we leisurely walked, engaged in animated conversation, and indulged in the classic boyish pastime of throwing rocks, little did we know that our usual track exploration was about to take an unexpected turn. I was just twelve years old at the time, and my oldest brother's keen eyesight caught something peculiar, something that stood out amidst our familiar surroundings. We were well acquainted with these tracks and could instantly tell when something didn't belong. Curiosity piqued, we continued walking towards the enigmatic sight, still oblivious to the significance of what lay before us.

In the waning light of the evening, it appeared to be nothing more than a large mound of black dirt nestled on the left side of the tracks, not far from the rails. Without giving it much thought, we approached it while engrossed in our chatter, absentmindedly kicking stones along the way. Drawing closer, perhaps within a range of 100 to 150 feet, an astonishing sight unfolded before our eyes, shattering our sense of normalcy. To our utter surprise, the mound abruptly stood up, towering on two legs—a colossal figure, easily reaching a height of 7 to 8 feet. With an incredible display of power, it effortlessly cleared a double set of railroad tracks in just two massive strides, swiftly vanishing into the depths of the wooded ravine on the right side of the tracks.

The magnitude of what we had witnessed struck us like a bolt of lightning. It was as if time had slowed down, imprinting every detail of that awe-inspiring moment into our memories. The creature we saw was undeniably tall, standing at a towering height of 7 to 8 feet, its imposing figure defying any logical explanation. Its upper body was massive and robust, leaving an indelible impression on our young minds.

In a surge of adrenaline-fueled terror, we instinctively turned on our heels and sprinted home as fast as our legs could carry us. Bursting through the door, we breathlessly recounted the encounter to our father, seeking solace and reassurance. As fathers often do, he offered a plausible explanation, assuring us that it was probably just a deer. In the moment, I accepted his explanation, despite the fact that I had never witnessed a deer standing upright on two legs, effortlessly traversing a double set of railroad tracks. However, even to this day, I cannot conclusively claim that it was indeed bigfoot that we encountered. The fleeting glimpse we caught of the creature didn't provide us with a clear view, nor did it emit any of the spine-chilling howls or distinctive sounds commonly associated with such encounters. Nevertheless, one thing remained undeniable—it was an entity unlike any animal we had ever seen before. Perhaps it was merely a man, but if so, he should have secured a place in the record books for his extraordinary abilities.

Allow me to paint a picture of the surroundings to give you a better sense of the setting. The area encompassed the railroad tracks, which were accompanied by gentle slopes and adorned with patches of grass and clusters of small bushes on the left side. On the right side, a stretch of woodland flourished, complete with a slight ravine adding depth to the landscape. There, nestled amidst the woods, you could find a small creek meandering its way alongside a serene pond, enhancing the natural allure of the area.

Once our father was notified of our astonishing encounter, he, like any concerned parent, listened attentively to our tale, offering both his support and a sense of rationality. But deep down, we knew that what we had witnessed that fateful evening went far beyond the realm of ordinary. It left an indelible mark on our young lives, forever fueling our curiosity and leaving us with a sense of wonder about the mysteries that lie just beyond the veil of the known.

ENCOUNTERS BIGFOOT

11

AN UNSETTLING ENCOUNTER

n the realm of the supernatural, my fascination has always been more theoretical than experiential. While I've delved into the mysterious and the eerie through books and films, real-life encounters with the paranormal had eluded me – until one fateful All Hallows' Eve. As an author of paranormal fiction, I'm known in my circle for spinning a good ghost story and orchestrating elaborate Samhain celebrations. These events have become a signature of mine, drawing crowds from near and far to our secluded estate for a night of thrills and chills.

Our property, nestled in a remote area far from the bustle of city life, serves as the perfect backdrop for our Halloween extravaganzas. We spend months preparing, turning every corner into a spectacle of horror and delight. The highlight for many is the midnight tour I lead through the eerie woods adjacent to our estate. It's a tradition that has become the centerpiece of our festivities, with guests eagerly anticipating the spine-tingling tales I weave under the moonlit sky.

This particular Halloween, however, introduced an element of genuine terror that I hadn't anticipated. Amid the usual fanfare, a lone figure caught my attention – a young man, seemingly out of place with his dated, non-costume attire. His presence was an anomaly; he didn't appear to be part of any group, and his detached demeanor set him apart from the lively atmosphere. What particularly unnerved me were his eyes – dark, deep, and unnervingly focused on me.

Trying to shake off the unease, I led the final group into the woods, but the sensation of being watched clung to me, intensifying with every step into the forest. The woods, usually a place of exhilaration for me, felt unfamiliar and threatening. Throughout the tour, I couldn't escape the feeling of a predatory presence lurking just beyond sight.

Returning to the festivities did little to dispel my fears. The mysterious young man had vanished, leaving me with a slew of unanswered questions. His absence only deepened the mystery and my unease. In the aftermath, I found myself drawn back to the woods, compelled to investigate and reassure myself. Armed with a flashlight, I ventured into the darkness, only to encounter the unnerving sight of two glowing orbs that I instinctively knew belonged to that same enigmatic visitor.

This encounter plunged me into a state of dread and obsession. The experience has left me grappling with the possibility that I may have unwittingly invited something otherworldly into my life. Despite my lifelong fascination with the paranormal, this brush with the unknown has left me questioning the nature of what I encountered and the implications it holds for me and my family.

The days since have been filled with sleepless nights and a haunting sense of foreboding. Theories about black-eyed entities offer some explanation, but I can't shake the feeling that what I encountered was something far more sinister. The excitement of having experienced a genuine paranormal event is overshadowed by a growing apprehension about what this encounter might mean for our future.

12

ECHOES OF THE NORTHERN CASCADES

Nature has been my sanctuary since childhood. Born and raised in the rugged terrain of northwestern Oregon, I was enveloped by dense forests, meandering rivers, and a rich tapestry of local legends. My early years were defined by hunting, fishing, and exploring these wild spaces, where I developed a deep connection with the outdoors. By the time I turned eighteen, I had become quite the experienced woodsman, familiar with the subtleties and secrets of the wilderness. It was against this backdrop that my best friend, Alex, and I concocted a plan for an adventure that would soon take an unexpected turn.

Our destination was the Northern Cascades in Washington State, a region famed for its breathtaking landscapes and mysterious folklore. This trip was not just a casual outing; it was a rite of passage, a test of our mettle against the untamed wild. Our excitement was partly fueled by our favorite TV show at the time, which had featured the Cascades' enigmatic beauty. We were eager to walk the paths of our screen heroes and delve into the mysteries of the Cascade Creature, a legendary being shrouded in myth.

Accompanying us were our girlfriends, Emily and Sarah. They were the perfect companions for this journey, sharing our sense of adventure and wonder. Our group was a close-knit quartet, bound by friendship and a mutual love for the great outdoors. The trip promised a blend of exploration, camaraderie, and perhaps a brush with the unknown.

We set off in the autumn of 2002, a time that now seems so distant and innocent. Our three-hour drive to the Cascades was filled with laughter, anticipation, and the kind of spirited conversation that only comes with youth and freedom. The cabin we rented was our base camp, a cozy haven in the midst of the vast, wild forest. It was the perfect setting for what we imagined would be an unforgettable adventure.

Our first night at the cabin was a snapshot of youth in its purest form. We played beer pong, listened to music on our old boombox, and shared stories under the starlit sky. Our bulky camcorder, a relic even then, was our window to the past, capturing these moments for posterity. Little did we know, it would soon become a crucial piece of our extraordinary experience.

The following day was our first foray into the wilderness. The forest of the Cascades was unlike anything we had seen. Towering trees, dense underbrush, and the constant murmur of hidden streams created an ambiance that was both awe-inspiring and slightly unnerving. Our goal was to explore, to find those spots immortalized by our favorite TV show, but nature has a way of making every tree, every rock look similar, disorienting even the most seasoned hiker.

As we ventured deeper, an eerie feeling crept over us. It was as if the forest itself was watching, its ancient eyes following our every step. We joked about the Cascade Creature, half in jest, half in genuine curiosity. Maybe, we thought, we were treading on sacred ground, disturbing spirits long at rest. But our youthful bravado pushed these thoughts aside, and we continued our trek, eager to discover what secrets the forest might reveal.

Our picnic in the heart of the forest was a moment of tranquility, a serene interlude amidst our exploration. We had brought simple fare – homemade sandwiches, fruits, and ample water. But this peaceful scene was abruptly shattered. Sarah's scream pierced the stillness, a sound so shocking it rooted us to the spot. She had been struck in the head by a stone, a large one that lay ominously close to our blanket. We scanned the surroundings, but there was nothing – no sign of who, or what, might have thrown it.

Dismissing it as a fluke, we tried to continue our meal, but the forest had other plans. Stones began raining down on us, an inexplicable, terrifying assault from an unseen adversary. Panic took hold, and we fled, leaving our belongings behind in our haste to escape.

Back at the cabin, we tried to make sense of the inexplicable. Theories abounded – from mischievous spirits to the elusive Cascade Creature. We were scared, yet there was an undeniable thrill in the unknown, a desire to understand what lurked in the shadows of the forest.

The next night brought new terrors. Emily's whispered warning in the dead of night was the prelude to an onslaught of sounds that seemed to come from everywhere and nowhere. The cabin shook under the force of heavy blows, and animalistic noises filled the air. We huddled together, a mix of fear and fascination holding us in its grip. When the tumult subsided, replaced by an eerie silence, we knew that our adventure had taken a turn into the realm of the unexplained.

The following morning, we returned to our picnic site, a scene of disarray and unanswered questions. Our food was gone, the cooler destroyed. It was clear that we were not alone in these woods, but who or what shared this space with us remained a mystery.

Determined to capture proof of our unseen visitors,

we set up our camcorder, hoping to catch a glimpse of the creature or creatures that had turned our adventure into a foray into the unknown. But the forest kept its secrets, and the next morning, we found the camera and tripod missing, leaving us with more questions than answers.

Our departure from the Cascades was filled with mixed emotions – relief, disappointment, and an unquenched curiosity about the mysteries of the forest. We speculated about what we had encountered – intelligent beings, perhaps a family of Bigfoots, curious and cautious in equal measure. Our experience in the Cascades remained an enigma, a tantalizing glimpse into a world just beyond our understanding.

In the years since, Alex and I have often reminisced about that trip, wondering if we should venture back, seeking answers to the questions that have lingered in our minds. The mystery of the Northern Cascades remains unsolved, a puzzle that continues to beckon us, inviting us to delve once more into its depths. If we ever return, I promise to share the tale of our quest for the truth hidden in those ancient, whispering forests.

13

SASQUATCH ENCOUNTER

During the early 1980s, my life took an unexpected turn when I accepted a position as a youth guide at a remote wilderness camp, designed for teenagers aged 12 to 15. Set in a picturesque but isolated location, the camp's environment resembled those seen in thriller movies - young, inexperienced staff and minimal adult supervision. For privacy reasons, I'll refrain from naming the camp, but it's worth noting that it's still operational, and the bizarre incident I experienced has turned into an almost mythical tale, often recounted during late-night gatherings.

I initially viewed this role as an easy way to bolster my college applications. It was a full-time commitment throughout the summer, where I was responsible for supervising outdoor activities for the campers. The camp was several towns away from my hometown, and I was unfamiliar with both the staff and the attendees. However, I've always had an easy time making friends and adapting to new environments. The era back then was much more relaxed, with lenient rules for everyone at the camp.

The staff arrived a week before the campers to prepare and bond with one another. The senior staff believed that this pre-camp bonding would foster a sense of camaraderie, essential for smooth operations with minimal supervision. There was an on-call adult in the main office cabin for emergencies, but largely, the camp functioned with the staff and campers left to manage on their own.

The cabins for staff were nestled deep in the woods. Since I owned a Jeep suited for off-road, I had permission to park it nearby, which was practical for emergencies. The living arrangements were gender-segregated, but everyone in the neighboring cabins was amiable and outgoing. Our first night was filled with stories and laughter around a campfire. Some local staff shared tales of mysterious entities in the woods, stirring a mix of skepticism and mild anxiety among us.

In the following days, we got acquainted with the camp's layout, safety protocols, and first aid - the only certification required of us. The centerpiece of the camp was a beautiful man-made lake, which I was particularly eager to explore. We were advised to always have a companion and to never wander alone, echoing the same rule to the campers for their safety.

Several days in, the camp routine was running smoothly. I had bonded well with the other staff members and even had an eye on a potential summer fling. One morning, finding myself without companions for a swim, I decided to bend the rules and drove my Jeep down to the lake. En route, I ran into Cheryl, another instructor headed the same way. Breaking yet another rule about unsupervised mixed-gender pairing, we decided to go to the lake together.

The day was perfect until an unsettling splash and a bizarre moaning noise echoed from across the lake. Initially dismissing it as other staff enjoying the lake, a sense of unease soon crept over us. The serenity of the day was shattered when the noises repeated, louder and closer than before.

To our disbelief, an enormous creature emerged from the lake, heading straight towards us. Its size was staggering, and it moved with an unsettling speed, emitting terrifying noises. In a state of panic, Cheryl and I made a split-second decision to swim back to shore, aiming for my Jeep. Cheryl reached the shore ahead of me and scrambled towards the vehicle. I was close behind, but the creature's thunderous approach was unnerving.

We barely managed to get into the Jeep, but in her frantic state, Cheryl crashed it into a tree. The creature, now on land, loomed over us, easily twelve feet tall. In a terrifying moment, it reached for Cheryl, trying to pull her out of the Jeep. Driven by fear and adrenaline, I struggled to fend off the creature. After a tense standoff, it released Cheryl, locking eyes with me momentarily before retreating into the woods.

We drove to the nurse's cabin, Cheryl in shock and injured. We concocted a story about a car accident to explain her injuries, but the nurse seemed to sense there was more to our tale. Soon after, Cheryl left the camp, deeply affected by the encounter.

For the rest of the summer, I was extra cautious, especially around the lake. This incident has stayed with me over the years, heightening my awareness during outdoor activities. Reflecting on it, I believe we encountered a creature resembling Bigfoot, considering the camp's location in a region known for such sightings.

This harrowing experience has made me acutely aware of the mysteries that may exist in the wilderness. It's a reminder of the unknowns that lurk in the shadows of nature. The incident at the lake has instilled in me a profound respect for the unexplained phenomena in our world, and I often ponder the fate of Cheryl and the true nature of the creature we encountered that fateful day.

14

THE MAIDEN OF THE MEADOW

As a child, my cousin and I often spent summers at our grandmother's home in western Kentucky. We hailed from a bustling urban center in Kentucky, so our visits to grandma's rural abode felt like entering a new realm. Our grandmother, a woman of the earth, had spent her entire life in that very home. Approaching her late eighties when she shared this particular tale, her mind remained razor-sharp despite her age. Our parents would dismiss her tales as mere fantasies of an aging mind, but my cousin and I would eagerly gather around the hearth each night, hanging onto her every word. Her home, lacking modern amenities like television, never failed to captivate us. The house, starkly different from its original state during grandma's childhood, once lacked basic facilities like indoor plumbing and electricity. It was a family home where generations lived and passed, leaving grandma as its sole inheritor. She raised our mother there, and we all sensed that she would one day pass away in this very house.

Nestled deep in a vast expanse of wilderness, the property was surrounded by dense forests and winding paths leading to a secluded pond. My cousin and I would spend entire summers there, relishing the freedom and simplicity of rural life. Once old enough, I took on the role of preparing our evening meals, after which we would gather by the fire to listen to grandma recount tales from her youth. Her stories, often about her adventures in the woods with her sister, were a fascinating window into a bygone era of simplicity and wonder.

Years have passed since grandma's departure, but her stories linger in my memory. I've taken it upon myself to document these tales, starting with one that still sends shivers down my spine. This particular story, shared by a woman of utmost integrity, remains an enigmatic and chilling memory. Now, as I bring my children to the house, now occupied by my parents, I find myself hesitant to let them wander near the pond. Here is the tale that planted the seed of unease in my heart.

As children, my cousin and I spent countless hours exploring the forests, playing games, swimming, and fishing in the pond. Around the time I was thirteen, and my cousin eleven, we concocted a plan to go night fishing – a novel and thrilling idea for us. We prepared our gear and eagerly approached grandma with our plan. However, she firmly forbade us from venturing near the pond after dark. Her uncharacteristic sternness puzzled and disappointed us, but we complied, opting for bed instead.

That night, after persistent questioning, grandma finally revealed the reason behind her strict rule. She sat between our beds in the dimly lit room and began a haunting tale from her youth.

Grandma and her sister, like us, were bound by the rule to be indoors by nightfall. They rarely ventured into the woods after dark, save for the occasional night fishing trips with their father. Those nights, according to grandma, were unnerving, filled with a sense of being watched, a sentiment her sister shared.

One night, long after they had gone to bed, a peculiar noise woke them. Accustomed to the nocturnal symphony of rural Kentucky, they recognized this sound as out of place. A woman's sobbing, interspersed with moans of pain, echoed eerily from outside their window. Paralyzed with fear, the sisters debated whether to investigate or seek their parents' comfort. Opting for the former, they cautiously approached the window but saw nothing, despite the cries sounding alarmingly close at times.

After about ten minutes, the sobbing ceased. They tried to return to sleep, but a lingering sense of dread kept grandma awake. She then felt a presence in the room and heard a faint sobbing. Terrified, she sensed a woman's voice whispering a prayer alongside her internal recitations. Suddenly, a dim light appeared near the door, and upon opening her eyes, grandma saw a small, illuminated figure in white.

This ghostly woman pleaded with grandma to follow her to the pond, urgently tugging at her arm. Despite her fear, grandma resisted, screaming out loud. The figure vanished instantly, taking the light with her.

The commotion woke her sister and soon their mother, who tried to calm grandma, insisting it was just a bad dream. Yet, the next morning, evidence of the encounter was visible on grandma's arm – bruises and scratches where the woman had grasped her.

Despite sharing this experience, grandma's family remained skeptical. However, she and her sister occasionally heard the crying woman again, choosing to ignore it. Over time, her sister came to believe the tale, but their parents never acknowledged it.

To this day, the mystery of the sobbing woman at the pond perplexes me. I've considered researching local history for clues but remain apprehensive. While nothing similar has occurred during our visits, the story continues to haunt me. Grandma's sincerity makes it all the more baffling and unsettling, leaving the true nature and intent of the ghostly woman a lingering question in my mind.

15

A NORTHERN FOREST MYSTERY

n my early teens, around fourteen years of age, I had a spine-chilling encounter with a creature that defies explanation. This wasn't a solitary experience; I wasn't the only witness, which confirmed it wasn't a figment of my imagination. The incident remains vivid in my memory, and I feel it's time to share it.

Back then, I lived with my family in a remote part of northern Minnesota. It was a tranquil and isolated world, far from the hustle and bustle of city life. The late 1980s were simpler times, especially in our secluded corner of the world. My younger brother Aaron and I would spend our days exploring the vast stretches of woodland that surrounded our home. Our parents, preoccupied with their daily struggles, seldom questioned our whereabouts as long as we steered clear of trouble.

Our closest friends, Leah and Jason, siblings like us, shared our adventurous spirit. Their home life was turbulent, much like ours, so they often found solace in our company and the escapades we embarked on. The four of us formed an inseparable bond, united by our mutual desire for escape and exploration.

Our routine was simple yet fulfilling. During school days, we would eagerly wait for the final bell, signaling the start of our adventures. We would trek through the woods, discover hidden trails, and share stories of local legends and folklore. Our destination was often the same - our grandmother's house, nestled about four miles away in an even more secluded area. The journey itself was an adventure, taking us through dense forests and over rugged terrain.

Our grandmother, a kind-hearted and gentle soul, lived alone since the passing of our grandfather. Her farmhouse, a relic of the past, stood as a testament to simpler times. She welcomed us with open arms, always prepared to feed our hungry stomachs and listen to our day's tales. For us, her home was a sanctuary, a place where we could be ourselves without judgment or fear.

The day of the encounter started like any other. Leah and Jason arrived at our place early in the morning, their faces beaming with the anticipation of the day's adventure. We set out on our dirt bikes, the cool morning air filling our lungs with a sense of freedom and excitement.

The path through the woods was familiar, each turn and landmark etched into our memories.

As we neared grandmother's property, we noticed something unusual at the top of the hill near her house. It was a figure, too distant to make out clearly, but its presence was enough to pique our curiosity. Grandma rarely had visitors, and certainly not on a weekday. We approached cautiously, our minds racing with possibilities.

What we saw upon closer inspection was beyond the realm of normalcy. The entity was unlike anything we had ever seen or heard of. It stood there, tall and slender, with a skin tone that seemed to blend with the natural surroundings. Its head was elongated, not unlike the fictional Coneheads, but with a more sinister aura. The creature's height was imposing, easily over eight feet, but what truly unnerved us were its arms. They were disproportionately long, hanging past its knees, almost touching the ground.

A sense of dread washed over us as we stood there, rooted to the spot. The creature's gaze seemed to pierce through us, and for a moment, time stood still. We were caught in a standoff, not knowing whether to approach or flee. The air around us felt charged, as if the very atmosphere was reacting to the creature's presence.

Without warning, the creature moved. It was a swift, fluid motion that seemed to defy the laws of physics. In a blink, it closed the distance between us, its long arms swaying eerily by its sides. Panic set in, and we scattered in different directions, our hearts pounding in our chests.

The creature's movements were erratic, almost playful, as if it was toying with us. It would dart towards one of us, then suddenly change direction and pursue another. We were like prey in a twisted game of cat and mouse, our screams echoing through the forest.

In a desperate attempt to escape, we split up, hoping to confuse the creature. I remember running as fast as my legs could carry me, the underbrush scratching at my skin, my breath coming in ragged gasps. Behind me, I could hear the others, their panicked shouts mingling with the sounds of the forest.

After what felt like an eternity, we regrouped at the edge of the woods, our bodies trembling with adrenaline and fear. We looked back, half expecting the creature to emerge from the trees, but it was gone. The forest was silent, as if holding its breath.

We didn't speak much as we made our way to grandmother's house. Our minds were still processing the surreal encounter, trying to make sense of what had happened. Grandma listened to our story with a mixture of concern and disbelief. She had lived in those woods for decades and had never seen nor heard of such a creature.

In the days that followed, we debated whether to tell

others about our experience. But who would believe us? A group of teenagers claiming to have seen a mythical creature in the woods? We decided to keep it to ourselves, a shared secret that bonded us even more.

Years have passed since that day, and I still find myself thinking about the creature. Was it a guardian of the forest, a spirit of the land, or something else entirely? The memory of its piercing gaze and the feeling of utter helplessness still haunts me.

I've scoured books and the internet, looking for any clue as to what we encountered that day, but to no avail. It remains a mystery, a puzzle piece that doesn't fit into the natural order of things.

Perhaps one day, the truth will come to light. But until then, the memory of the long-armed creature in the northern woods will continue to linger in the back of my mind, a reminder of the mysteries that lie hidden in the shadows of our world.

16

ECHOES FROM THE BLUE RIDGE

Back in the 1980s, my lifelong friend Alex and I shared a bond akin to brothers. Our childhood in rural Pennsylvania was marked by countless adventures, especially since we grew up in an era before the ubiquity of cell phones and digital cameras. Those were simpler times, when a camera was a bulky, special-occasion gadget, not a daily carry item. This detail is crucial because, whenever I recount the eerie events that unfolded in our youth, people inevitably ask why we didn't capture any of it on film. But in those days, film was a precious commodity, and you never knew if your shots would turn out clear or not.

Our tale begins in our teenage years, a period when our lives started taking different paths. The woods behind our houses, once our playground, saw us less as we got engrossed in the typical teenage preoccupations of cars and dating. However, for Alex's 19th birthday, we decided to revisit our childhood haunts – the mysterious woods and the enigmatic caves in the nearby town of Millville, a place that had always sparked our imaginations.

The caves, known among the locals as "The Whispering Caverns," were part of the Blue Ridge Mountain Park's sprawling landscape. Our earlier visits as children, under the watchful eyes of our parents, had only given us a glimpse of their potential for adventure. But now, armed with the independence that comes with age and a car – my trusty old Ford Pinto – we planned a weekend of exploration, free from parental oversight.

We packed our supplies – some food, a couple of flashlights, and a hearty dose of teenage bravado – and set off towards the caves. These caverns were steeped in folklore, with tales dating back to the late 1800s. Local legend had it that a hermit named Jonathan Clark once made these caves his home, giving them their mystique and ominous name. The story went that Clark, an eccentric loner, had ventured here from the distant Appalachians and spent his final years in the labyrinthine depths of these caverns.

The motel where we checked in was a modest establishment, about a half-hour's drive from the caves. It was the kind of place that would be the perfect setting for a spine-chilling horror story – isolated, rundown, and seemingly forgotten by time. Our room was at the very end of a row of identical units, bordered by a thick, foreboding forest that seemed to whisper secrets in the wind.

From the outset, there was an air of unease about the place. It might have been the way the trees swayed under the moonlight or the way the motel's neon sign flickered intermittently, casting eerie shadows. Despite the chill that ran down our spines, we settled in, planning to start our adventure early the next morning.

However, the first night at the motel turned out to be anything but restful. Stepping outside for a cigarette – a habit we had picked up in our rebellious phase – we were immediately struck by the profound silence of the night, broken only by the distant hooting of an owl. But then, an unsettling noise cut through the stillness, a high-pitched, keening sound that seemed to come from the depths of the woods. It was unlike anything we had heard before, a chilling blend of a wail and a screech that made the hairs on the back of our necks stand up.

As we stood there, frozen, the lights of the motel flickered and dimmed, casting long shadows that danced across the ground. We hurried back inside, bolting the door behind us. Despite the alcohol coursing through our veins, sleep eluded us, as strange scratching and whispering sounds seemed to echo around the room.

The next day, trying to shake off the unease from the

night before, we set out for the caves. The Whispering Caverns were more than just a geological wonder; they were a maze of legends and unexplained mysteries. We were determined to explore the parts of the caves that were off the beaten path, the sections that were not meant for tourists' eyes.

Our journey through the caves was an exercise in both awe and fear. The formations within were breathtaking, with stalactites and stalagmites creating an otherworldly landscape. But as we ventured deeper, away from the marked paths, the air grew colder, and the oppressive silence of the underground pressed in on us.

It was in one of the more remote caverns that we first heard it – a sound that chilled us to our bones. It was the same keening wail we had heard the night before, only now it was accompanied by a sense of something ancient and malevolent lurking just beyond the reach of our flashlights. We tried to convince ourselves it was just the wind or some animal, but deep down, we knew it was neither.

Panic took hold as the sounds seemed to close in on us, echoing off the cave walls. We scrambled back towards the entrance, the noises following us, growing louder and more frenzied. It wasn't until we emerged into the night air, gasping for breath, that the sounds abruptly ceased.

But the respite was short-lived. As we made our way back to the car, the forest around us seemed to come alive with whispers and rustling, as if the trees themselves were speaking in hushed, conspiratorial tones. Our flashlights cast long, menacing shadows as we hurried along the path, every snapped twig and rustled leaf sending jolts of fear through our bodies.

It was then, in the clearing by the car, that we saw it – the source of our terror. A creature, humanoid but grotesquely distorted, stood at the edge of the light cast by my headlights. Its skin was pale and stretched tight over its bony frame, its limbs long and twisted. But it was the hands that truly horrified us – elongated and ending in sharp, rake-like claws.

The creature moved towards us, its movements jerky and unnatural, as a cacophony of whispers filled the air around us. Its eyes, small and black, seemed to bore into our very souls. In that moment, we understood that we were in the presence of something utterly inhuman, a creature of nightmares made flesh.

Without a word, I turned the key in the ignition, and we sped away from the creature and the Whispering Caverns, leaving behind a mystery that would haunt us for years to come. In the years that followed, I would learn of the legend of The Rake, a creature of folklore that seemed to match the horror we had encountered.

But knowing its name did little to ease the memory of that night, a night when the shadows of the Blue Ridge Mountains revealed a terror beyond our wildest imaginings.

17

MYSTERIOUS ENCOUNTER WITH A MOUNTAIN GIANT

n the brisk autumn of 1983, at the age of twenty-four, I found myself living a life full of zest and adventure. My home was a quaint hamlet nestled in the heart of the Rocky Mountains, a place where privacy was a rare luxury and community ties were strong. I was on the cusp of marrying Laura, the girl who had been my neighbor and childhood sweetheart. We were both only children and had spent our formative years side by side. Our homes were located in a well-to-do area of the village, but it was the surrounding dense forests that truly captivated our hearts. We had spent countless hours exploring these woods, becoming intimately familiar with their secrets and wonders. Our relationship had blossomed at the age of fifteen and had flourished ever since, much to the delight of our parents, who were themselves close friends.

Growing up, Laura and I were no strangers to the great outdoors, having been on numerous camping and hiking excursions with our families. Laura had a profound love for animals, often rescuing injured wildlife, which we would nurse back to health together. These moments, though sometimes heart-breaking, strengthened our bond. This story, however, centers around a peculiar and chilling incident that occurred during our first camping trip as a couple, without the company of family or friends. Unbe-knownst to Laura, I had planned to propose to her during this excursion. I had confided in my mother about my intentions, and although she swore secrecy, I suspected she might have hinted at it to Laura's mother, judging by the knowing looks we received as we set off into the wilderness for a planned five-day adventure.

Our destination was a secluded cabin in the moun-tains, complete with modern amenities including a hot tub. We were well-prepared with supplies for both our stay at the cabin and our explorations of the nearby forest. Although we had been to this general area before, this particular section was new to us. I had chosen a picturesque spot beside a serene lake, surrounded by the vibrant colors of fall, as the location where I intended to propose. Our first evening was spent in the comfort of the cabin, enjoying a homemade dinner and relaxing in the hot tub. We eagerly anticipated the next day's picnic by the lake.

The following morning, we embarked on our hike, planning to conclude it with our picnic. However, an eerie sensation soon enveloped us, a feeling of being observed and followed. This unnerving presence lingered as we navigated the woods, occasionally inter-rupted by unexplained noises and periods of unsettling silence. Upon reaching the lake, its beauty was undeni-able, but the sense of being watched intensified.

After about an hour at the lake, the distinct sound of footsteps on the forest floor snapped us out of our reverie. Despite scanning our surroundings, we saw no one. This mysterious presence felt increasingly ominous. I stood up, feigning possession of a weapon, and demanded the unseen observer reveal themselves. Part of me even fantasized that our parents might be secretly witnessing what they believed would be a proposal.

As we prepared to leave, the situation escalated. Venturing a short distance into the woods to investigate, I was startled by the sudden appearance of a massive figure, roughly ten feet from me. It emitted a bizarre, guttural sound, reminiscent of a fictional character from a famous space opera. Initially, it appeared to be a man in a bulky suit, but as I observed more closely, I realized it was a creature unlike any I had ever seen. It stood at least eight feet tall, covered in long, brownish-red hair, interspersed with leaves and twigs. The stench it emitted was overpowering.

Laura, hearing the noise, joined me, and the creature's behavior became more aggressive. Its eyes, unnervingly human-like in their appearance, conveyed a mixture of curiosity and menace. It growled menacingly, taking a few steps in our direction. The realization hit us that this creature had likely been tracking us since our arrival, with Laura as its primary focus.

In a panic, we retreated, with Laura momentarily stopping to grab our picnic basket. I urged her to leave it, and we ran back to the cabin. Notably, the creature did not chase us but instead let out a series of mournful howls, suggesting an emotional depth that was unexpected and unnerving.

Back at the cabin, our conversation revolved around this harrowing experience. In those days, tales of mountain giants were relegated to myths and legends, often used by parents to caution their children in the wilderness. But our encounter was very real, forever altering our perception of the unknown.

Despite the encounter, we remained in the area for the duration of our trip. I proposed to Laura the next night, amidst the romantic setting of the cabin's hot tub, and she joyfully accepted. This moment of happiness helped us momentarily forget the fear we had experienced.

Our love for nature didn't wane after this incident, but we became more cautious. We never returned to that particular area of the forest, and thankfully, never encountered any other mysterious creatures. In retrospect, I wish I had captured a photograph of the creature, but at the moment, our safety was my only concern. With the advent of the internet and the rise in popularity of cryptozoology, I've come to realize that our encounter was not unique. Many have reported similar experiences with these elusive giants of the mountains, each story adding to the tapestry of mystery surrounding these creatures.

18

AN UNEARTHLY ENCOUNTER

n the midst of my thirties, grappling with the storm of a disheartening divorce, life had cornered me into a phase of introspection and solitude. The echoes of my failed marriage led me to seek shelter in my Uncle Gerald's home, nestled in a quiet suburban neighborhood. The walls of my life seemed to close in, suffocating my spirit, and the thought of escaping to a distant, serene place, preferably amidst nature's embrace, frequently crossed my mind. My heart ached for solace, an escape from the relentless grip of reality.

During this turbulent phase, an unexpected call from a long-lost friend, Alex, pierced the monotony of my life. We had been the epitome of friendship in our school days, virtually inseparable, sharing dreams and adventures. But life, as it often does, steered us onto divergent paths post-graduation. Alex ventured into academia and later into a world of affluence and success, while I remained rooted in our hometown, embracing the simple, unadorned life of a mechanic.

Alex's call came as a surprise, a pleasant anomaly in the era of the late nineties where digital communication was still in its nascent stage. His voice, a blend of warmth and concern, reached out to me, offering a respite from my current woes. He spoke of a secluded retreat in the heart of a forest, a place where the cacophony of the world faded into a tranquil silence. It was an invitation to rekindle our friendship, to find solace in the lap of nature. The opportunity felt like a ray of hope, a chance to escape the shadows that loomed over my life.

With a heart filled with anticipation and a mind clouded with uncertainty about our altered lives, I embarked on the journey. The drive was long, stretching over eight hours, leading me into the embrace of the wilderness. As I navigated through familiar roads and unknown trails, memories of our past adventures with Alex flooded my mind, bringing a mix of nostalgia and apprehension. Would our friendship withstand the test of time and the changes it had brought?

The retreat was a spectacle of luxury, an oasis of opulence amidst the rustic wilderness. The main lodge stood majestically, a grand structure of elegance and extravagance, contrasting starkly with the simplicity of the surrounding nature. I was a stark anomaly in this lavish setting, my worn jeans and calloused hands a testament to a life of labor and simplicity.

The cabin, arranged by Alex, was a marvel in itself. Its interiors were adorned with luxury, from a lavish massage table to a heated pool, exuding a sense of extravagance that was both overwhelming and awe-inspiring. It was a stark reminder of the divergent paths our lives had taken. Alex's greeting was warm and heart-felt, dissolving any lingering fears of our friendship having succumbed to the changes in our lives. He showed me to the loft, an open, airy space that would be my haven for the duration of our stay.

The following morning dawned bright and clear, the forest cloaked in a pristine blanket of snow. Alex and I embarked on a hike, the crisp air filling our lungs, the tranquility of the woods offering a much-needed respite from the turmoil within. As we traversed the forest trails, Alex shared his own trials, mirroring my own struggles with divorce and the complexities of life. It was a moment of solidarity, a realization that despite our different journeys, our cores remained connected by shared experiences and emotions.

Our conversation was abruptly cut short when Alex's gaze fixed on something behind me, his expression morphing into one of intrigue and caution. He motioned for silence, and we cautiously ventured off the beaten path, following his line of sight into the deeper, uncharted parts of the forest. The sense of unease grew within me, a premonition of something unknown and possibly dangerous lurking in the misty woods.

That's when we saw it – an enormous figure, shrouded in the shadows of the trees. It stood towering and imposing, exuding an aura of primal strength. Its sudden, ear-piercing roar shattered the silence, sending a wave of terror through my body. We turned and ran, the creature's angry growls echoing behind us, a terrifying soundtrack to our frantic escape.

At the bottom of a hill, we stopped, panting and disoriented. The creature had halted its pursuit, and in that eerie calm, a brilliant light cascaded from the sky, illuminating the figure before it receded back into the shadows of the forest. The source of the light was a sight to behold – an egg-shaped, metallic craft, hovering silently above. The craft was an enigma, defying the laws of physics and nature, and then, just as mysteriously as it had appeared, it ascended into the night sky and vanished.

Back at the cabin, Alex and I processed our encounter, a mix of disbelief and wonderment. We were convinced we had witnessed not just a forest guardian, a creature of myth and legend, but also an extraterrestrial craft, an unidentified flying object. The connection between the two remained a puzzle, an intricate web of possibilities that defied logical explanation.

Our story, though met with skepticism and disbelief, remained a profound experience that bonded us in a unique way. The lodge's front desk clerk was the only person who showed a flicker of belief, hinting at deeper secrets hidden within the forest. Reports of similar sightings in the area, both before and after our encounter, suggested a hidden world, a realm where the lines between the natural and the supernatural blurred.

Years have passed since that winter day in the misty woods, but the memory remains vivid, an unexplained chapter in our lives. The encounter raises questions about the mysteries of our world, the unseen forces that reside in the shadows of our understanding. It stands as a testament to the infinite possibilities that the universe holds, a reminder that sometimes, reality can be stranger than fiction.

19

ENTITY IN THE FIELD

t was the year 2009, and I found myself employed at a tedious manufacturing facility located on the edge of a diminutive village in Eastern Iowa. My role entailed working graveyard shifts, which, while inconvenient in timing, were generally straightforward and uneventful. The workforce was small, so the environment was often quiet, with only the sound of machinery breaking the silence. My peers and I, a group of young men in our mid-twenties, often resorted to lighthearted antics to make our shifts more bearable. This particular night, however, was destined to be different. Shortly before my shift began, I received a call from a colleague, informing me unexpectedly that no shipments were due to arrive that night – an unprecedented situation. Curious and hoping for a night off, I called my supervisor, but he insisted I report for duty and find other ways to keep busy. Resignedly, I headed to work.

Upon my arrival, I tidied my work area and the machinery, but it didn't take long before I ran out of tasks. With nothing else to do without stepping on others' toes, the vastness of the facility became more apparent and somewhat unsettling. It seemed only two other colleagues had shown up, which added to the night's strangeness. Perhaps the others, having heard the same news, had decided to stay away. They were smarter than I was, choosing freedom over an empty night at work. Boredom led me to the rear loading docks for a cigarette, where I watched the night sky and the occasional bat.

The factory was encircled by an enormous barley field, a sea of golden stalks that stood nearly as high as my shoulders. At around three a.m., as I stood there, something unusual in the field caught my attention. It wasn't typical wildlife movement; it was something more, something that stirred a sense of unease within me. Driven by curiosity and a touch of nostalgia for my childhood adventures in similar fields, I decided to investigate. There's something inherently calming about being in the midst of nature, even under such peculiar circumstances.

I ventured into the field, guided by the limited light emanating from the factory's floodlights. I hadn't informed my colleagues of my excursion and wasn't sure where they were at the time. Intending to circle back in about an hour, I followed existing paths through the barley. However, I soon sensed that I was not alone.

Ahead of me, a shadowy figure moved. Initially, I thought it might be a deer, common around these parts, but the notion quickly dissipated. A sudden chill overcame me, and I was seized by an inexplicable dizziness and nausea. Nonetheless, my curiosity propelled me forward. The figure resembled a small child, and concern for its wellbeing overrode my apprehension. Following it seemed like the right thing to do at the moment.

Chasing the figure, dressed in a dark garment, through the field felt surreal. After a short pursuit, it disappeared into the darkness. The situation grew more unnerving, and my instinct urged me to return to the factory. But then, the sound of childish laughter echoed behind me. Despite my fear, I couldn't ignore the possibility of a child in danger. My calls were met with silence, and with a heavy heart, I decided to head back.

As I neared the loading dock, I noticed that the lighting had changed – one floodlight was out, and the other dimmed significantly, a change that must have occurred while I was in the field. The atmosphere felt oppressive, and a sense of heightened alertness overcame me. Then, the eerie laughter resounded again, this time surrounding me with a malevolent tone. I confronted the source at the field's edge, demanding it reveal itself.

What I saw was a creature of small stature, with unkempt black hair and ragged clothes. Its face, unnaturally pale, was dominated by oversized, pitch-black eyes. It grinned at me, revealing sharp, uneven teeth. Its movements were erratic and disjointed, as if it were struggling against an unseen force. Inside, a voice screamed for me to flee.

I turned and ran back to the safety of the factory, hearing a beastly howl behind me. Upon reaching the dock, both floodlights were functioning perfectly, and the field appeared normal. My coworkers noticed my agitated state when I re-entered. I brushed off their concern, claiming illness, and slept until my shift ended.

For years, I kept that night's encounter to myself, rationalizing it as a figment of stress or exhaustion. But curiosity eventually led me to research similar phenomena. Stories of "The Pale Crawlers," often sighted in fields like the one behind my workplace, emerged. Despite working there for another half-decade, I never experienced anything like that night again. Nor did I hear of others encountering such a creature. Sharing this story now, I hope to connect with others who might have witnessed these beings and to find some understanding of that mysterious night in the barley field.

20

THE MYSTERIOUS VISITOR IN THE SNOW

My earliest memories are set in a remote hamlet, surrounded by miles of countryside. As an only child on a secluded farm, I often felt the pangs of loneliness. Our nearest neighbors were several miles away, making playtime with friends a rarity, dependent on our parents' availability to drive us. This tale begins in the 1970s, a period not particularly plagued by safety concerns, but the sheer distance to my nearest playmate's house was a significant barrier. The landscape was dotted with a few isolated homes, yet they did little to shrink the vast distance between us. This narrative marks the beginning of a series of encounters with a peculiar entity, encounters that spanned my entire life. Initially, this presence made itself known only during heavy snowfalls, remaining an outdoor specter. However, its appearances began to intrude indoors after we got a television, always materializing in the dead of night. To my knowledge, no one else has encountered this being, or if they have, they've kept it to themselves. My first encounter with it occurred during an intense snowstorm, which led to emergency-level conditions and left several feet of snow in its wake. At that time, I was ten years old, and the remoteness of our home made school attendance impossible even if it had been open.

Our farm, more of a relic than a functional agricultural site, had seen its days of cultivation long pass. My father worked in a nearby workshop, and my mother was a full-time homemaker. At that point in my life, I was the sole child, though I would later have a handful of siblings. On the day the snowstorm subsided, life began its usual rhythm. The morning was filled with the smell of my mother's cooking and the routine of bidding my father farewell as he left for work. After eating, I played in my room while my mother busied herself with chores. The snow-covered outdoors seemed to beckon me, and I longed to play in it. I asked my mother to join me, but her household responsibilities prevented her. After some insistence on my part, she allowed me to venture outside alone, with the condition that I remain visible from the kitchen window. I agreed eagerly, excited to enjoy the snow-covered backyard.

My initial experience outside was idyllic. I built a modest snowman and enjoyed the quiet serenity of the snow-laden surroundings. My love for nature was evident; I frequently explored the dense woods that bordered our farm. However, curiosity got the better of me, and I ventured towards the woods, contrary to my mother's instructions. That's when I noticed something unusual.

Walking towards the woods, which were a good distance from the house, I spotted a figure at the edge of the forest, motioning to me. It looked human but strangely indistinct, as though out of focus. My mind initially thought of a neighbor, but I quickly dismissed this as improbable. Driven by curiosity, I continued towards it. As I got closer, an inexplicable sense of dread and fear gripped me, and I stopped in my tracks. The figure was unusually tall, humanoid, and its appearance was akin to a noisy television screen – a sight I was unfamiliar with at the time, as television was a new addition to our home. A voice, clear yet sourceless, called my name, urging me to come closer and claiming my mother had given her permission. Despite my apprehension, I was strangely compelled to approach.

Reaching the entity, I was baffled by its form: a human outline filled with a static-like substance, resembling a hastily sketched cartoon character. It gestured for me to follow it into the woods, and I found myself obeying. As we moved deeper into the forest, it communicated with me telepathically, reflecting my interests in a bid to gain my trust. However, my mother's voice, laced with anxiety, echoed through the trees, snapping me out of my trance. The entity's demeanor instantly changed, its face morphing into an angry, cartoon-like expression. Frightened, I shouted for my mother, and just as quickly, the entity disappeared, leaving no footprints in the snow.

My mother reprimanded me for venturing out of sight but was also visibly relieved to find me safe. I kept the encounter with the entity to myself, but later learned of several children in the area who had mysteriously vanished while playing outside. The realization that I had narrowly escaped a similar fate was chilling. I referred to the being as the "static visitor," a secret I've maintained to this day. Now, as an elderly person, I still see it occasionally slipping in and out of the television screen, but I choose to ignore it, a strategy that seems to keep me out of harm's way.

———

Continue with Mysteries in the Forest: Volume 2

ABOUT THE AUTHOR

Erik Lake, a pen name adopted to maintain privacy, is a seasoned author with a deeply-rooted passion for the mysteries of human culture and the unexplained. Prior to embarking on his writing career, he served as a professor of anthropology at a prestigious university, where he was celebrated for his captivating lectures and scholarly publications. His academic pursuits led him across the globe, from the jungles of the Amazon to the mountainous terrains of the Himalayas, in search of understanding the complexities of human behavior and tradition.

Throughout his academic tenure, Erik developed a keen interest in folklore, myths, and the stories that often go untold or are overshadowed by mainstream narratives. It was this curiosity that led him to explore themes of the paranormal and the enigmatic phenomena that challenge our understanding of reality.

Since leaving academia, Erik has devoted himself to full-time writing, specializing in works that merge his anthropological background with topics often considered too taboo or unsettling for conventional scholarly dialogue.

Erik Lake brings to the literary world a rare blend of academic rigor and open-minded curiosity. Whether he's shedding light on cryptids, spirits, or age-old legends, his works provide a well-balanced blend of skepticism and wonder, prompting readers to question their own beliefs and perspectives.

Away from the pen and paper, Erik enjoys hiking, amateur photography, and spending time with his family in a quaint, undisclosed location surrounded by nature's untamed beauty. Yet, the woods for him are not just a retreat but an ongoing field of research—a labyrinth of endless questions and bewildering phenomena that continue to fuel his prolific writing career.

ALSO BY ERIK LAKE

THINGS IN THE WOODS

BEYOND THE PATH

FROM ABOVE: UFO ENCOUNTERS

WENDIGO CHRONICLES

ALSO BY FREE REIGN PUBLISHING

WENDIGO CHRONICLES

MYSTERIES IN THE FOREST

Printed in Great Britain
by Amazon

58818304R00078